Corporal Works of Mercy
Mercy in Action

by
Mgr Richard Atherton

All booklets are published thanks to the generous support of the members of the Catholic Truth Society

CATHOLIC TRUTH SOCIETY
PUBLISHERS TO THE HOLY SEE

Contents

Mercy in Action 3

"Whatever you did to the least of my brethren..." ... 10

Feed the Hungry & Give Drink to the Thirsty 18

Clothe the Naked & House the Homeless 22

Visit the Imprisoned & Visit the Sick 26

Bury the Dead 32

The Spirituality of the Seven 39

Endnotes..................................... 44

All rights reserved. First published 2015 by The Incorporated Catholic Truth Society, 40-46 Harleyford Road London SE11 5AY Tel: 020 7640 0042 Fax: 020 7640 0046. © 2015 The Incorporated Catholic Truth Society.

ISBN 978 1 78469 080 9

Mercy in Action

I do not think there is a Gospel phrase which has made a deeper impression on me...than this one: "Insofar as you did this to one of the least of these brothers of mine, you did it to me". One has only to think that these words were spoken by the uncreated Truth, who also said, "this is my body...this is my blood".[1]

The kindly American

In spring 1986 two grey-haired men met and greeted each other warmly. Their last meeting had been forty years earlier. Then they had met as enemies. Then their meeting had been in a dark cave in Okinawa. Now they met in the bright lights of Tokyo's International Airport. And this time they met as friends. One was Japanese, Ishibasi, the other an American, a former sergeant, Ponich.

In 1946 in the mouth of a cave in Okinawa, Ponich was holding a young Japanese boy in his arms; the five-year-old youngster had been shot through both legs. When Ishibasi and his colleague, both of them snipers, suddenly leaped out of the dark recesses of the cave where they'd been hiding and confronted the American with guns raised and about to fire, the situation seemed hopeless. But Ponich gently laid the boy on the ground, took out his first-aid kit, and began to clean the wounds. As he humbly explained later, he could think of no better way of preparing for death that by an act of mercy.

But his act of mercy begot another. The snipers, amazed at what they'd seen, slowly lowered their rifles. Ponich took up the child in his arms, bowed in gratitude to the two Japanese, and carried the boy to a field hospital. Four decades later he wrote to a Tokyo newspaper, belatedly thanking the Japanese people because two of their soldiers had once spared his life. Ishibasi read the letter and contacted the newspaper, and so the meeting with Ponich was arranged.[2]

The kindly American "could think of no better way of preparing for death than by an act of mercy". At any time, mercy is the form that love takes in the face of human distress. And so God, who *is* love, is also mercy. Mercy is, if we can put it this way, in his DNA! The Polish nun Sr Faustina, whom Pope St John Paul II called "the great apostle of Divine Mercy in our time", wrote in her diary that God's mercy is "the greatest and highest of the divine attributes" and is "divine perfection pure and simple".[3] Those bold words only re-echo all that the Bible has to tell us.

"God of mercy and compassion"

In the Old Testament God is revealed to Moses as "merciful and gracious...abounding in steadfast love and faithfulness"

(*Ex* 34:6). The Hebrew words used to describe the bond between God and his people suggest that God's mercy is one of loving faithfulness: it is like the love of a mother for the child of her womb, it is utterly dependable. Chapter 11 of Hosea, one of the highpoints of Old Testament theology, pictures God as a doting parent, whose patience has been tried to the limit by rebellious children; the temptation to punish may be strong, but infinite compassion prevails, because, says the Lord through his prophet: "I am God and not mortal"; human mercy at its best is but the palest shadow of the divine mercy. The psalmist proclaims over and over again that "his love [a word which also means 'mercy'] has no end" (*Ps* 136). God is always ready to hear the cry of the poor and come to relieve them in their distress. God is their rock, their shield, their fortress. As the Jewish scholar Abraham Heschel would have said: Israel's God is not characterised by apathy, but by its opposite, *pathos* (passion) - by passionate concern for humanity, by intimate involvement in the life story of God's people. The Exodus, the deliverance of Israel from slavery, is God's loving, merciful response to his people in their time of dire distress. It is the paradigm and pattern of human need and divine deliverance: in that sense, it stands as a summary of the whole Bible. Inevitably, it calls for a response from God's people: they too must be merciful, especially to the poor, to the marginalised, to widows and orphans who are otherwise without support.

"The face of the Father's mercy"

In the opening words of the official Bull that announced the Holy Year of Mercy, Pope Francis reminded us that "Jesus is the face of the Father's mercy";[4] he is the revelation of what our God is really like; in him "the loving-kindness (the tender mercy) of the heart of our God…visits us" in person (*Lk* 1:78). And so the gospels offer overwhelming evidence of Jesus's compassionate response to human suffering and need: he heals the sick, cleanses lepers, casts out devils, feeds the hungry, and touches the 'unclean' and allows them to touch him; he is moved to tears at the death of his friend; he even raises the dead to life. Just as one of the words used for mercy in the Old Testament is linked with the maternal womb, so one in the New Testament links it with a person's innermost being; in each case there seems to be an attempt to express the inexpressible, the limitless depth of compassion with which God is moved by human need: the divine compassion is almost something physical.

"I have set you an example"

Jesus not only shows forth the mercy of God, he also urges his followers to do the same: "Show mercy," he says, "just as your Father shows mercy" (*Lk* 6:36). On the night before he died he performed the lowly service which was normally left to a slave: he knelt and washed the dust-covered feet of his disciples. Then he told them: "…you also ought to wash one another's feet. For I have set you an example, that you should do as I have done to you" (*Jn* 13:14-15). We must not be like the wicked servant in the parable who, having been freed of an enormous debt by his generous master, then failed to show compassion to a fellow servant who owed him a paltry sum (*Lk* 7:41-42). Similarly, the message of the famous parable of the Good Samaritan is that we are called upon to be good neighbours, compassionate neighbours, by coming to the aid of whoever stands in need of our help (*Lk* 10:30-35).

Above all, in his majestic description of the Last Judgement Jesus makes it clear that our eternal fate is bound up with how we have helped, or failed to help, those in need. The 'needs' in questions are all of a bodily, corporal, nature: food and drink for the hungry and the thirsty; clothes and a home for those who are without them; visiting of those who are sick and those who are in prison; and burying of the dead. Jesus came not to save souls but to save people, and people are bodies as well as souls. And so while there are "Spiritual Works of Mercy" (see the companion CTS booklet of that title) there are also Corporal Works of Mercy, which are our particular concern here.

The sheep and the goats

Jesus says:

> "When the Son of Man comes in his glory and all the angels with him, then he will sit on the throne of his glory. All the nations will be gathered before him, and

he will separate people one from another as a shepherd separates the sheep from the goats, and he will put the sheep at his right hand and the goats at the left. Then the king will say to those at his right hand, 'Come, you that are blessed by my Father, inherit the kingdom prepared for you from the foundation of the world; for I was hungry and you gave me food, I was thirsty and you gave me something to drink, I was a stranger and you welcomed me, I was naked and you gave me clothing, I was sick and you took care of me, I was in prison and you visited me.' Then the righteous will answer him, 'Lord, when was it that we saw you hungry and gave you food, or thirsty and gave you something to drink? And when was it that we saw you a stranger and welcomed you, or naked and gave you clothing? And when was it that we saw you sick or in prison and visited you?' And the king will answer them, 'Truly I tell you, just as you did it to one of the least of these who are members of my family, you did it to me.' Then he will say to those at his left hand, 'You that are accursed, depart from me into the eternal fire prepared for the devil and his angels; for I was hungry and you gave me no food, I was thirsty and you gave me nothing to drink, I was a stranger and you did not welcome me, naked and you did not give me clothing, sick and in prison and you did not visit me.' Then they also will answer, 'Lord, when was it that we saw you hungry or thirsty or a stranger or naked or sick or in prison, and did not take care of you?' Then he will answer them, 'Truly I tell you, just as you did not do it to one of the least of these, you did not do it to me.' And these will go away into eternal punishment, but the righteous into eternal life" (*Mt* 25:31-46).

St James, that most down-to-earth of men, sums it all up in a sentence: "there will be judgement without mercy for those who have not been merciful themselves; but the merciful need have no fear of judgement" (*Jm* 2:13).

"Whatever you did to the least of my brethren..."

On the night of the Last Supper, Jesus made two extraordinary statements. First, he told his disciples: "as the Father has loved me, so I have loved you" (*Jn* 15:9); and then, "as I have loved you, so you also must love one another" (*Jn* 15:12). It is as if God's compassionate love is being compared to a huge waterfall, descending from its source in the Father, becoming incarnate in the Son, and finally waiting upon us to allow it to reach out to our brothers and sisters everywhere. The Church is infinitely more than "a kind of social or charitable agency; as the Body of Christ, it is the sacrament of the continuing effective presence of Christ in the world";[5] as members of the Body, each one of us has a personal responsibility to share in the mission of the Lord of Mercy. Blessed Mother Teresa was expressing the same thought when she said that "welfare is for a purpose - an admirable and a necessary one - whereas Christian love is for a person. The one is about numbers, the other about a man who was also God".[6]

The Seven Corporal Works of Mercy

Of course the list of seven Corporal Works of Mercy is not meant to be exhaustive: today there are many other activities that would fit into the same category, such as caring for the earth or fighting against abortion or taking action against global warming or working for nuclear disarmament or putting an end to the scourge of human trafficking. Of the seven 'official' Corporal Works of Mercy, six come straight from our Lord's Last Judgement scene. The final one seems to have been added later. It reflects the horror that Jews felt when anyone was left unburied: it's a horror shared almost universally today. Tobit, the author of the biblical book that bears his name, records how in times of persecution he would bury the dead in secret at the risk of his life: "I performed many acts of charity to my kindred…if I saw the dead body of any of my people thrown out behind the wall of Nineveh, I would bury it. I also buried any whom King Sennacherib put to death…in his anger he put to death many Israelites; but I would secretly remove the bodies and bury them…Then one of the Ninevites went and informed the king about me, that I was burying them; so I hid myself…Then all my property was confiscated; nothing was left to me…except my wife…and my son…" (*Tb* 1:16-20).

Inspiration and encouragement

In the following pages we'll meet men and women who exemplify the various Corporal Works in outstanding fashion. These exceptional individuals are meant to inspire and encourage, but not to overawe us, making us feel that we are unable to compete with them. We don't need to compete; there is no competition. Our great God is also a God of little things. No act of kindness to a neighbour, however small it may be, goes unnoticed by the Lord. Did not Jesus himself promise that those who give "a cup of cold water" to one in need would "not lose their reward" (*Mt* 10:42)? That is why after each of the sections dealing with the individual Corporal Works of Mercy a special piece will be added, entitled "Nearer home". It will point to ordinary people who illustrate humble ways in which we can rise to the challenge of the Corporal Works of Mercy; it will also suggest some, though by no means all, of the modest ways in which we all might serve the Lord in the least of his brothers and sisters.

The tradition of the Seven Corporal Works

The practice of the "Seven Corporal Works of Mercy", as they came to be called, runs like a golden thread through the history of the Church since its earliest days. St Paul attests to it by his zeal in making collections in his communities scattered about the Mediterranean world to help their poverty-stricken sisters and brothers in Jerusalem (*Ac* 24:17; *1 Co* 16:1; *Gal* 2:10). According to Tertullian, a famous African theologian of the third century, it amazed the pagans, who commented: "See how these Christians love one another".[7] We catch a glimpse of it in the story of St Lawrence who was martyred in 258. He was a deacon with special responsibility for the poor and needy in the city of Rome. When persecution broke out and the Roman Prefect ordered him to reveal where the Church's treasure lay hidden, he brought the official to a gathering of the poor and sick of the city and announced: "Here is the Church's treasure".

The charitable work of the Church

Once the Church gained imperial protection, at the beginning of the fourth century, charitable work could be conducted more openly and in fact became widespread. Through the deacons the bishop would oversee the work in his diocese, the presbyter (or parish priest) in his parish. Many of these deacons had medical knowledge and some were the equivalent of modern day nurses. The first General Council of the Church, at Nicea in 325, decreed that every city should have its hospital; often enough these hospitals made special provisions for people suffering from leprosy. One of the most famous city hospitals, close to Notre Dame Cathedral in Paris, was known, significantly, as *Hôtel-Dieu* (hostel of God). The names of some of the oldest and best-known hospitals in England bear witness to their Christian origin: St Thomas's, for example, was named after St Thomas à Becket; and Bart's, built in response to the vow made by a man on pilgrimage to Rome and staffed for centuries by Augustinian monks and nuns, was named after St Bartholomew. In churches during the Middle Ages the Corporal Works of Mercy were sometimes depicted in paintings or in stained glass windows to remind worshippers of their duties as followers of Christ. Monks, nuns and deacons provided many of the services for those in need which are nowadays supplied by the Welfare State. The fact that the senior female nurse in the wards of our hospitals today is called "Sister" is a tribute to the work of nuns throughout the ages in caring for the sick and disabled.

Vincent de Paul

The seventeenth century witnessed the life and mission of St Vincent de Paul (1581-1660) who has been called the "Great Apostle of practical charity", and is honoured as a saint in the Anglican Communion as well as in the Catholic Church. Born into a peasant family in Gascony, Southern France, he became a priest at an extremely young age but within a decade had discovered his true calling - to give himself unstintingly to the poor for the rest of his days. He saw Christ present in those whom he served and urged his followers to reverence and love them: "Let us work," he told them, "with a new love in service of the poor, looking for the most destitute and abandoned among them. Let us recognise that before God they are our Lords and masters, and we are unworthy to render them our small services". On another occasion, aware of the danger of demeaning those who would be on the receiving-end of their charity, he pointed out to his community: "The poor will forgive you for giving them bread, only because of your love". He strove to improve the lot of galley slaves and eventually became their chaplain, he preached missions in prison, he gathered a group of wealthy women who collected money for his many missionary projects and he set up the Congregation of the Mission, often known as Vincentian Fathers, to evangelise the poor and assist in the formation of the clergy.

Serving the poor

In 1633, together with his friend Louise de Marillac, he founded "the Daughters of Charity". As a congregation, they were unique in that, unlike other religious sisters at that time, they were to be 'unenclosed', living in the world in the midst of those they served; the streets of the city would be their cloister, the homes of the sick their monastery. They would serve in hospitals and on battlefields, in the slums and in institutions for the disabled, in fact wherever there was sickness, poverty, suffering or need of any kind. And their motto would be: "The love of Christ urges us on" (*2 Co* 5:12).

Less than two centuries later, inspired by the example of St Vincent de Paul, Frederic Ozanam, a young married layman, born in Milan and brought up in Paris, helped to set up what came to be known as the St Vincent de Paul Society (or SVP).[8] It was a society dedicated to tackling poverty and disadvantage by offering practical assistance to those in need - irrespective of faith, ethnicity, age or gender. Ozanam was a brilliant scholar and devout Christian who, through association with the poor and disadvantaged, found himself being transformed, being sanctified. It led him to view society from the perspective of the people who are excluded, to become more compassionate and caring, and to a deep commitment to the elimination of poverty and suffering. The Society which Fredric and his companions founded in 1833 spread quickly and is now to be found throughout Europe and beyond. When in August 1997 Pope St John Paul II beatified Fredric he explained that before the 1939-45 War he had himself been a member of the SVP. Today there are few parishes in the UK that are without the familiar SVP box, which awaits donations from the faithful that will enable members of the SVP Conference to serve the poor of the parish in whatever ways they can: by assisting the needy and the housebound, by visiting hospitals and prisons, by providing furniture for those who have little of their own.

Mercy in the modern Church

The Second Vatican Council (1962-65), which presented the most up-to-date expression of the Church's understanding of herself and her mission, stated unambiguously: "…there is an inescapable duty to make ourselves the neighbour of every individual, without exception, and take positive steps to help a neighbour…whether that neighbour be an elderly person, a foreign worker who suffers the injustice of being despised, a refugee…or a starving human being who awakens our conscience by calling to mind the words of Christ: 'As you did it to one of the least of these my brothers or sisters you did it to me' (25:40)".[9]

When Pope St John Paul II canonised Sr Faustina, the saint of God's mercy, in 2000, he noted that she was the "first saint of the new millennium", the implication being that he hoped that appreciation of God's mercy, and our response to it, would be the striking features of the Church in the twenty first century. And now we have Pope Francis who supplies sleeping bags for the homeless and showers for them in the Vatican; who never tires of speaking about God's mercy; whose first book is simply called "The Church of Mercy"; and whose social encyclical *Laudato si'*, which has the plight of the poor at its heart, has met with almost universal acclaim. There can be little doubt that the Church's commitment to the Seven Corporal Works of Mercy is as resolute today as it has been at any time in her long history.

Feed the Hungry & Give Drink to the Thirsty[10]

Food and drink are among our most basic needs. In the western world, where shops are piled high with foodstuffs and where, at the twist of a tap, a plentiful supply of water is readily available at any time, it is hard to visualise a situation where every day is virtually a life and death struggle for food and water. As Archbishop Romero powerfully stated: "It is not God's will for some to have everything and others to have nothing".

Mary's Meals

In the early nineties, over a bottle of beer, two brothers were watching a TV news bulletin about the appalling sufferings of the people in war-torn Bosnia. There and then they decided to take a week off work to see how they might be able to help. It began with a long, long journey in a battered old Land Rover; it ended with one of them, Magnus MacFarlane-Barrow, the father of a large family and already deeply involved in charity work, making a momentous decision.

A few years earlier, while visiting Malawi, he had met a young boy whose family lived in extreme poverty, and the youngster had told him that he dreamed of having enough to eat and being able to go to school. Now Magnus realised what he must do: he resolved to encourage children to come to school by providing them with a meal each day; feeding of body (food) would go hand in hand with feeding of the mind (education). Selling his house and giving up his job, and assisted by the generosity of innumerable people - as well as, as he humbly admits, several "miracles" - he devoted himself full-time to the task. It led to the creation of "Mary's Meals" - Magnus had been inspired by his visits to Mary's shrine at Medjugorje; the new organisation would aim at providing chronically hungry children with one meal every day before they set off for school and so encourage them to embark upon an education that would help to lift them out of poverty in later life. Magnus MacFarlane-Barrow has published a book called *The Shed That Fed a Million Children*,[11] the 'shed' referring to the small shed in Dalmally, Argyll, where Magnus asked for donations for his initial trip to Bosnia-Herzegovina; and 'a million children' referring to the milestone of feeding a million children every school day. That milestone was reached in May 2015, leading Magnus to remark that while this achievement should be celebrated, it still leaves another fifty-seven million children in need of help, and so "in some ways our work has only just begun".

Nearer home

To practise the first two Corporal Works of Mercy we don't have to go off to far-away lands. Taking a hot dinner to an elderly neighbour, helping in a local soup kitchen, making a contribution to a food bank, asking the local MP to use his influence to ensure that the hungry are fed and the thirsty given drink both at home and abroad, making a donation to Mary's Meals, reading Magnus's book, taking the time and trouble to learn more about the problem of hunger and thirst in various parts of the world - these are some of the ways in which we can respond to our Lord's appeal.

We can support missionary priests and sisters who have first-hand knowledge of people's needs in various parts of the world because they share them. Often they are at the forefront of schemes to alleviate the problems of their people; for example, they have encouraged plans for the sinking of wells - sometimes assisting in the work with their own hands - so that a supply of clean, fresh water is made available to everybody. Again, we can give our support to organisations such as CAFOD, the official aid agency of the Catholic Church in England and Wales. It owes its birth not to bishops or priests or politicians but to two lay women from the Catholic Women's League who organised the first Family Fast Day on 11th March 1960. Two years later CAFOD was officially registered and since then its outstanding work for the underprivileged has become known and admired throughout the world and its Family Fast Days have become part of parish life. Fasting, even if it's only a matter of eating or drinking a little less than usual, enables us in some small measure to share the experience of our sisters and brothers in the developing world.

Live simply

Climate change is one of the great threats of our time and, with its legacy of droughts, floods and hurricanes, it is much more damaging to the poor and underprivileged than it is to the wealthy. Many parishes have shown great ingenuity in adopting the three principles of the "LiveSimply" scheme initiated by CAFOD, that is by living in solidarity with people in poverty; by living simply; and by living sustainably with creation. However overwhelmed we may feel in face of the challenge of climate change, we are not helpless: we can all do something to express our care for creation and love for our neighbours, from emailing politicians, to saving energy at home or at church, to spreading the word of what we are doing to others who might join our efforts.

Clothe the Naked & House the Homeless

All human beings deserve a coat for their back and a roof above their heads. Clothes afford protection from the elements and are a sign of respect for human dignity; a home gives identity and security and a sense of belonging. 'Crisis' is the national charity for single homeless people in England. Its chief executive wrote recently: "Homelessness is devastating, leaving people vulnerable and isolated." Evidence that was presented before the Supreme Court in May 2015 indicated that the average life span of homeless men and women is just forty-seven; they are over nine times more likely to commit suicide and thirteen times more likely to be a victim of violence than the rest of the population.

Throughout the ages the Church has cared for those who are without proper clothing and a home. Religious sisters have fed and clothed and provided a home for countless children, and adults, in all parts of the world, and of course are still doing so today.

The Ark

For more than fifty years L'Arche communities - there are over 130 of them spread across the globe - have served people with intellectual disabilities, many of whom previously suffered in dehumanising institutions, by providing them with a family-like home and an atmosphere conducive to their human growth. They offer a welcome to people of all religions, making it their aim to support each person in his or her own faith tradition. Their founder is Jean Vanier, internationally recognised for his humanitarian work, which extends to other marginalised people, such as prisoners, the homeless and those who are abandoned. He says that the Beatitudes have been his inspiration.

Born of Canadian parents in 1928, Vanier served first in the British and then in the Canadian Navy but, looking for a deeper meaning to life, resigned his commission to devote time to prayer and the study of philosophy. After a short spell of teaching in Toronto University, he returned to France; there a priest friend, Father Thomas Philippe, invited him to visit an institution for people with intellectual disabilities. Jean was so distressed by their plight and so moved by their desire for friendship that he bought a small house in the village of Trosly-Breuil and invited two men to join him there. It became their family home and they named it "L'Arche", after Noah's Ark, the craft that saved people from disaster. Other L'Arches quickly followed and soon young people, inspired by this new way of living in community, came to help; these 'assistants' became part of the 'family' and quickly discovered, as Jean had already done, that those they befriend are a source of personal growth to themselves, helping them to see what is most important in life. Jean Vanier by his words and still more by his actions re-echoes the sentiments of St John Paul II, who wrote: "Let us keep the sick and handicapped at the centre of our lives. Let us treasure them and recognise with gratitude the debt we owe them. We begin by imagining that we are giving to them; we end by realising that they have enriched us."

Nearer home

There are many charities that help to provide homes for the homeless; they benefit from financial support and from the assistance of volunteers. Local politicians can be urged to support the building of affordable homes and ensure that refugees are housed decently. The pressure that ordinary people can exert on those who make decisions should not be underestimated. Before May 2015 local councils in England had to decide who, especially among young people, were 'vulnerable' enough for housing help, though how they should make that decision was far from clear. After a long-running legal battle, spearheaded by Crisis and its supporters, who included many MPs, the Supreme Court finally ruled that single homeless people will no longer have to prove they are particularly vulnerable compared to other homeless people in order to qualify for support. This decision should prove a blessing for many youngsters who sleep rough night after night.

Practical words and actions

In parishes that run a marriage training course there will normally be a professional who can offer practical advice to young couples about how to go about buying their first home. And of course parents, in financial or other practical ways, often help a son or daughter who is about to get married - though they may not recognise that by helping their children to get settled in a home they are also fulfilling one of the Corporal Works of Mercy!

As for clothing the naked, perhaps we are all being invited to look through our wardrobes to see if there are clothes hanging there that we have seldom or never worn. They could be offered to a charity shop and so would not only provide cheaper clothing for those who need it but also support for the particular charity to which the shop is connected.

Visit the Imprisoned & Visit the Sick

One of the earliest accounts of the Sunday celebration of the Eucharist, dating from about AD 150, records how there was a collection which was handed over to the celebrant, who then "gives aid to…such as are in want by reason of *sickness*…; and to those also that are *in prison*…in fact to all who are in need".[12]

We can readily understand why visiting the sick is numbered among the Corporal Works of Mercy, but may have difficulty in appreciating why prisoners, too, are deserving of our concern. It is not a question of 'going soft' on crime but of making the vital distinction between crime (or the sin) and the criminal (or the sinner). As Jean Vanier explains in the first of his "Five Principles of Humanity": "All humans are sacred, whatever their culture, race, religion, whatever their capacities and incapacities, whatever their strengths and weaknesses may be." It is good to see that in more recent times an increasing number of people - laymen and women, religious sisters and priests - are involved in visiting the sick and the imprisoned.

Good Pope John

When on an October evening in 1958, the portly and lovable Angelo Giuseppe Roncalli - soon to be known throughout the world as 'Good Pope John' - heard the outcome of the papal election, he summed up his feelings in a two-word Latin quotation taken from the book of Job: "Horrefactus sum". He was horrified, or, to put it more colloquially, he was shattered. Yet, only a few hours later, he was suggesting to his secretary that he should visit the large Regina Coeli prison on the outskirts of Rome on the very next day. Gently, it had to be pointed out to him that there were one or two other things that a new Pope might have to do first!

In fact, it was not until Christmas time that he managed to fulfil his plans. As he stood before his prisoner audience, he assured them that he came as "Joseph your brother" and told them that a couple of his own cousins had been "inside" and yet had come to no lasting harm. He had no prepared script but revealed his own deep feelings when he announced: "I want my heart to be close to yours, I want to see the world through your eyes". (Today, a plaque bearing that message is affixed to the wall of the Regina Coeli prison.) Many of his congregation, including prison officers as well as prisoners, were moved to tears, as he spoke. A convicted murderer fell on his knees before him, begging: "Holy Father, can there be forgiveness for the likes of me?" By way of reply Pope John raised him to his feet and embraced him; it was like a lovely re-enactment of the parable of the prodigal son.

Journalists may have expressed surprise that a Pope should go prison visiting, but he, as he noted in his diary, saw himself as simply fulfilling one of the Corporal Works of Mercy, which the gospel expects of all Christ's followers.[13]

Nearer home

'Visiting' the sick means much more than paying a visit to our dear ones when they are in hospital, though sadly even that duty is sometimes neglected. It may mean driving a frail elderly person to Mass on Sunday; or dropping in on neighbours who are chronically sick and offering help; or inviting them into our own home for Christmas dinner; or volunteering to help with Meals on Wheels; or making a phone call to a friend who is suffering from depression. In innumerable ways we can fulfil the injunction of visiting the sick. As a rule it will not demand specialised knowledge, but what it always does demand is perseverance and compassion; a genuine human caring presence; a listening ear, a loving heart and a genuine smile.

Paradoxically, some of the most vital and demanding 'visitings' of the sick may take place in our own homes, such as looking after elderly relatives who can no longer care for themselves, or tending a child who is seriously disabled but who is living at home with his or her parents. More and more these days, it seems, men and women have the task of caring for partners who suffer from dementia, who appear to have lost many of the qualities once most admired in them, who constantly repeat themselves, who no longer recognise their own husband or wife. This is the kind of 'visiting' that requires endless patience and whose value depends on such simple 'human' things as the gentleness of a loved one's touch, the care and deep concern vibrant in their voice, the calming influence of their presence. All this "embodied love" is, as Fr Daniel O'Leary has written, "the sacrament of invisible grace…the gospel fully lived".[14]

Write a letter

Even in prison, wonders are sometimes worked by human friendship which gives the prisoners a sense of their worth and value. That is why prison visiting by volunteers is part of life in most penal establishments, and many men and women are involved in this special ministry. In 2000 "Human Writes" came into existence, its purpose to provide pen-pals, from many parts of the world, for prisoners awaiting execution on Death Row. Jon Snow, broadcaster and patron of the organisation, has said that this simple mechanism of letter writing has had "a wonderful record of keeping hope alive" in the grimmest of circumstances.

In the early 1960s two Sisters of Charity and a chaplain entered through the huge entrance gates into Walton Prison. The Sisters, who ran St Vincent's School for the Blind and Partially Sighted, were facing a problem: some of their pupils were well able to take advantage of further education but if they went to 'sighted' colleges they would need Braille text-books; but in fact such books did not exist. What was to be done? The sisters had come to the prison in the hope of persuading a few prisoner volunteers to learn Braille so that they could then transcribe books for the blind children. It was a success story: not only did the youngsters get all the books they needed in Braille - at least two of them went to Oxbridge and one became president of the Union - but the prisoners themselves benefitted enormously: they were proud to have been able to help the children and, as one of them wrote later in a newspaper article, work for blind children had proved the best rehabilitation he had ever known.

Changing attitudes

In the United States, Charles 'Chuck' Colson, known as the 'hatchet man' in President Nixon's circle, was sent to prison in connection with the Watergate affair. While in prison he had a conversion experience which sparked a radical change in his life; on his release he founded Prison Fellowship which has since spread throughout the world including the UK. It aims at helping prisoners to reform and has won support from Christians of all the major denominations. There are over one hundred prayer groups of Prison Fellowship in this country which hold prisoners and their families before God in prayer.

A vital part of 'visiting the imprisoned' is the attitude we adopt towards prisoners and, above all, towards their families. A prison governor, who often gives talks about his work, once asked me: "Why is it that Christian audiences are almost always more punitive than any others?" I had no answer. But it is sad that followers of Jesus Christ should aim more at punishing than reforming, or should fail to recognise that imprisonment itself is the punishment which wrongdoers bring on themselves; and that loss of freedom is a punishment whose bitterness few can understand who have not experienced it themselves.

Encouraging rehabilitation

One of the most difficult tasks for the ex-prisoner is settling down to normal living on their release. So much depends on how they are received by the community, and also on whether or not they can find work. One employer always has some ex-prisoners in his workforce; he treats them as he treats his other employees and realises that this is his way of responding to this Corporal Work of Mercy.

The prophet Jeremiah, alarmed at the way children often suffer because of the failures of their parents, had the biting comment: "The parents have eaten sour grapes, and the children's teeth are set on edge" (*Jr* 31:29). It is a comment which could equally be applied to the children of prisoners: many of these youngsters, though innocent, are often treated badly, made to feel inferior, sometimes shunned by neighbours. Yet, these are just the youngsters who should receive special understanding in school and in their home neighbourhoods. No child and no family should be penalised because of the failure of one family member.

Bury the Dead

On 5th September 1997, within a few days of the tragic death of Princess Diana, another death was announced, which brought sadness to many people, especially the poor, in all parts of the world. It was the death of a small Albanian nun, Mother Teresa of Calcutta, who had died at the age of eighty-seven, after spending virtually the whole of her adult life serving the poor, the neglected, the destitute and the dying.

Mother Teresa

Born of peasant stock in the Yugoslavian town of Skopje, she had felt the call to serve the poor when she was only twelve years old. Six years later, having decided that she should become a missionary in India, she joined the Loreto Order. The Sisters ran a mission station in Calcutta and for some seventeen years she taught there in the girls' school. But already she had caught a glimpse of the dire poverty and squalor of the slums, of sick people who remained untended, of lonely men and women lying down to die in the streets, and of thousands of orphaned children wandering around with no one to care for them. In September 1946, while travelling by train for her annual retreat, she experienced what she later described as "the call within the call". "I was to leave the convent," she explained, "and help the poor while living among them."

And so in 1948, leaving behind the sheltered world of the convent and the fashionable girls' school, she went to live and work amidst the dirt, disease and stench of the slums, After a brief period of hospital training as a nurse, she became immersed in her missionary work among the poor, replacing her Loreto habit with a simple white cotton sari decorated with a blue border. Initially, she started a school in Calcutta, but was soon tending to the needs of the destitute and starving. In 1949, she was joined by a group of young women and the foundations of a new religious order, the Missionaries of Charity, was laid: it would exist to help the "poorest among the poor". Their first hospital, which had been donated to them by a Hindu official, consisted of a few rooms attached to a temple of the Hindu goddess Kali. There they accepted the poor, whatever their religion or lack of it.

Caring for the uncared for

Before they obtained a more suitable conveyance, it was not unknown for Teresa and her Sisters to be seen trundling a dying person though the streets in a wheelbarrow.[15] There might be nothing they could do to prolong life, but they wanted to do all they could to ease this person's sufferings; to wash them and feed them, if they were able to take food; and above all to enable them to die with dignity, knowing that they were loved and respected. As Mother Teresa explained: "The biggest disease today is not leprosy or tuberculosis, but rather the feeling of being unwanted, uncared for".[16] Great care was taken to offer the dying the rituals of their own faith, and so for Hindus there was water from the Ganges for their lips; for the Moslems, readings from the Koran; and for the occasional Christian, the last rites.

Her outstanding work earned her awards without number, including the prestigious Nobel Peace Prize which was awarded her in Oslo on 10th December 1979. In her acceptance speech she recalled:

"that man whom we picked up from the drain, half-eaten with worms, and we brought him to the home - [he said,] 'I have lived like an animal, but I am going to die like an angel, loved and cared for'…it was so wonderful to see the greatness of that man who could speak like that, who could die like that without blaming anybody, without cursing anybody… Like an angel - this is the greatness of our people."[17]

"Let's do something beautiful for God"

The late Malcolm Muggeridge, British journalist, author and media personality, who knew Mother Teresa and her work at first hand, wrote: "For me, Mother Teresa of Calcutta embodies Christian love in action. Her face shines with the love of Christ on which her whole life is centred, and her words carry that message to a world which never needed it so much." Muggeridge, whose book on Mother Teresa was one of the first reports to make her work widely known, chose as the title of his book an expression which, he said, he had often heard her use: "Let's do something beautiful for God". And in that book Muggeridge wrote: "Doing something beautiful for God is, for Mother Teresa, what life is about".[18]

Nearer home

According to a recent poll, sixty per cent of people hope to die at home; but in fact sixty per cent of us are more likely to die in hospital or in a similar facility. And so there is little chance that we shall be called upon, literally to "bury the dead". Nonetheless, this final Corporal Work of Mercy does make its demands upon us. There is the duty of visiting the dying, especially those who are specially dear to us, simply being with them, perhaps holding their hand, or, since hearing is the last lost of all the senses, speaking a gentle word or a brief prayer in their ear. In my mind's eye I see an elderly man sitting beside the bed of his wife; she is on her final journey in this world, and a long, difficult journey it has been. He sits beside her in silence, his hand holding hers; she can do nothing for herself; she is unable to see and scarcely able to speak. I know that this good man has made these visits over and over again week after week over the course of several years. And I know that what I am seeing is true love, what I am seeing is the final Corporal Work of Mercy in action.

Comfort the bereaved

If we have the spirit of 'burying the dead', then we'll see it as a duty not only to help our relatives and friends in any way we can in the time leading up to their death but also to ensure that they have a fitting burial, and that if they are Christians they have the attention of a priest. But even after the burial we haven't finished 'burying the dead'. There are still the broken hearts of the bereaved to be cared for. If we can strike up a patient friendship with those who have lost a dear one throughout their time of mourning, no matter how long that might take, we will have played an important part in easing their grief. Again, where Christian people are involved, we can often bring them great solace by arranging for Mass to be celebrated for their deceased loved one, or even by writing a letter, or sending a card, of condolence. In some parishes there is a specially trained group or men and women who are ready to minister to people who are going through the mourning process; in other parishes, members of the Legion of Mary or of the SVP or some other church organisation will go and say a Rosary in the home of the dying or of those recently dead. Many people have the lovely practice of praying each day for all the faithful departed.

Protect the meaning of life

In our day when 'assisted death' - or more precisely, 'assisted suicide' - is talked about more insistently than ever, we need to consider what we can do to ensure that human life is treated as sacred until it reaches its natural end. Nothing could be more contrary to the merciful work of 'burying the dead' than the work of bringing about their death. We may be able to enlist the support of our MPs on this issue, or become involved more directly by, for example, writing an article on the subject for a local newspaper. More importantly, each of us is inevitably helping to form public opinion; what we convey to others about this vital matter in the course of ordinary conversations is having its effect one way or another.

Care for the dying

One of the most powerful ways of offsetting the calls for assisted dying is by supporting the wonderful work of the hospice movement. Dame Cicely Saunders, nurse, medical social worker, doctor and surgeon, is the founder of the modern hospice movement, which has now spread across the world. Aware of the inadequacy of the care offered to the dying in most hospitals, she set up St Christopher's Hospice in the 1960s. There she pioneered research on pain control as well as on palliative care. She knew that a dying person is more than a patient with symptoms to be controlled: excellent medical care must be accompanied by 'holistic' support that takes account of a patient's practical, emotional, social and spiritual needs. She saw the dying person and the family as the unit of care, and she developed bereavement services to extend support beyond the death of the patient. Cicely Saunders was a devout Anglican and all that she did was underpinned by her strong Christian faith.

Finally, in regard to this work of mercy as in regard to the others, we all have it in our power to pray and by our prayers to win the support of the Lord, who by word and deed first taught us the vital importance of the Seven Corporal Works of Mercy.

The Spirituality of the Seven

Reflecting on the Corporal Works of Mercy, we may be struck by their sheer 'ordinariness'; the fact is that an eternity of importance can lie hidden in simple everyday actions. The Corporal Works may of course be practised in extraordinary, even heroic, ways, as we have seen already, but in themselves they are what might be expected of decent men and women who have a modicum of the "milk of human kindness" in their hearts; they might even be described as "doing what comes naturally". So, for example, good parents in the everyday care of their little ones - providing them with a home, with food and drink and clothing, and caring for them when they are sick - are already fulfilling at least five of the Corporal Works - even if they (the parents) don't realise it themselves! Indeed, in the Last Judgement scene, Jesus points out that both those who are blessed and those who are cursed will ask the same question: When did we see *you* hungry or thirsty or naked or sick or in prison? And the answer will be that whenever you did (or failed to do) any one of these things for the least of my brothers and sisters, you did (or failed to do) it to *me*.

"You will find God there"

Nonetheless, these actions will be spiritually more beneficial if they are done in accordance not simply with the words of the various Corporal Works of Mercy but also with their spirit, so that we perform them with some awareness of the Lord whom we are serving. That in turn means that we will do them with compassion and love for the Lord and for our brothers and sisters. In that way, simple daily activities become charged with special value and more and more our lives become genuine "spiritual worship" (*Rm* 12:1). Because he was so convinced of that truth, St Vincent de Paul assured his Sisters: "Ten times a day you will go to serve a poor person, and ten times a day you will find God there." Similarly, Mother Teresa often dealt with people who were so ravaged by the effects of hunger, disease and neglect that they were scarcely recognisable as human beings; yet she beautifully described each one of them as "Jesus in his distressing disguise."[19] We may not have the spiritual sensitivity of a Vincent or a Teresa, but at least we could pause from time to time to remind ourselves that many of our routine activities are service of God and our fellow men and women. We could also follow the example of those people who have the habit of praying each day the "Morning Offering", a prayer in which they express the desire that all their actions of this day (even if there is little time to reflect upon them in the busy-ness of life) may be to God's glory.

The Mother of Mercy

These reflections on the Seven Corporal Works of Mercy would not be complete without mention of our Mother, Mary, whom we address in one of our best-known hymns in these words: "Hail, holy Queen, Mother of Mercy". She is the Mother of Mercy for several reasons: firstly, because, through her immaculate conception, she is created as the masterpiece of the Lord of Mercy himself; secondly, she is the Mother of Mercy because she brought into our world Jesus, who is Divine Mercy made man, Divine Mercy made tangible; and thirdly, she is the Mother of Mercy because, even though the Scriptures offer us only fleeting glimpses of her life on this earth, yet they are sufficient to show that she exemplified the charism of mercy to a wonderful degree; and she did so vividly aware that she was serving her Son, even in the least of his sisters and brothers.

Roll up your sleeves!

After the annunciation (*Lk* 1:26f.), when she was already carrying the Christ Child in her womb, Mary's first recorded action was to hasten to visit her elderly cousin Elizabeth, who, she had just heard, was herself expecting a child (*Lk* 1:39f.). It was an errand of mercy; we can safely assume that on arrival at her cousin's, Mary didn't simply sit around, but rather rolled up her sleeves, ready to offer whatever help she could. And cannot we also safely assume that that readiness to help others was a feature of her hidden life in Nazareth? It was during her visit to Elizabeth that she proclaimed her song of praise, the *Magnificat* (*Lk* 1:46f.), in which she glorified God whose "mercy is for those who fear [reverence] him from generation to generation", "who has brought down the powerful…and lifted up the lowly" and who helped "his servant Israel in remembrance of his mercy". No wonder Mary's prayer has been a source of inspiration to many of the poorest and most neglected people in the world.

At hand to help

When her little One was born in Bethlehem (*Lk* 2:1f.), she did for him what any mother does for her child - she fed him and clothed him, kissed him and put him to bed, gave him a home, looked after him, taught him to walk and to talk and to say his prayers. Eight days after his birth, she named him "Jesus" (*Lk* 2:21f.), as she had been bidden to do by the Angel: it was a name which was based on the saving work which, in his mercy, he would accomplish for the human race. At the marriage feast in Cana (*Jn* 2:1f.), it seems that Mary was the first to notice, and be concerned, that some of the guests were without drink, and it was she who successfully interceded for them with her Son. While she seems seldom to have enjoyed her Son's company once his public ministry had begun, she must have been made aware, through reports coming to her from various quarters, of the miracles he worked, the stories he told, the messages he gave, the impact that he was having, the opposition that was building up against him. And when his life was drawing to a close, and the great act of sacrifice was about to take place, she was at hand. She had the bitter experience that no parent should have to endure, that of being present at the death of her Son - and this was a death hideous and humiliating almost beyond belief; she knew personally the unique torment of those who share the suffering of a dear one while feeling unable to do anything to alleviate the loved one's pain. It seems ironical that when her own dear Son cried out in his anguish "I thirst", Mary who had once nourished him at her breast and had won a miraculous supply of drink for the sake of the wedding guests at Cana, could do nothing now but stand by, helpless and broken-hearted.

Her eyes of mercy turned towards us

And finally, just as Mary had once laid her little Son in a manger, so now she fulfilled the final Corporal Work of Mercy for him, as she laid his lifeless body to rest in the tomb. Now her direct work for her Son was over; henceforth, she serves him in the least of his brethren. She more than anyone else can turn "her eyes of mercy towards us" and show us how, through the practice of the Seven Corporal Works of Mercy, we too, in our own small ways, can do "something beautiful for God".

Endnotes

1. J. F. Six (ed.), *Spiritual Autobiography of Charles de Foucauld* (Denville, New Jersey, Dimension Books, 1964) p. 147.
2. William J. Bausch, based on his *A World of Stories* (Mystic, Conn., Twenty-third Publications, 1998) p. 313.
3. W. Kasper, *Mercy* (New York, Paulist Press, 2013) p. 7.
4. Pope Francis, *Mericordiae Vultus*, Bull of Indiction of The Extraordinary Jubilee Of Mercy, §1.
5. Kasper, n. 3 above, p. 157.
6. Malcolm Muggeridge, *Something Beautiful for God: Mother Teresa of Calcutta* (London, Collins, 1971) p. 28.
7. Tertullian, *Apology*, chapter 39 (c.150).
8. A Fagan, *Through the Eye of a Needle* (St Paul's Publications, 1989).
9. *The Church in the Modern World*, § 27.
10. Since six of the Seven Corporal Works of Mercy seem to be linked to each other in pairs, we shall deal with them in that way.
11. M. McFarlane-Barrow, *The Shed That Fed A Million Children* (London, Collins, 2015).
12. *The First Apology of Justin Martyr*, lxvii (italics added by the author).
13. R. Atherton, *Summons to serve* (London, Geoffrey Chapman, 1987) pp. 53-4 (slightly amended).
14. Fr Daniel O'Leary, "Silent Grace of Forgetting", *The Tablet*, 12 October 2013.
15. Kathryn Spink, *Mother Teresa* (Harper One, revised edition) p. 25.
16. Muggeridge, n. 6 above, p. 73.
17. Spink, n. 15 above, p. 326.
18. Muggeridge, n. 6 above, p. 125.
19. Muggeridge, n. 6 above, p. 97.

Mercy Works

Mark P. Shea

The spiritual and corporal works of mercy are not a list to be learnt but actions to be lived. Mark Shea gives great examples of people who have performed the works of mercy and advice on how we can practice them in the 21st Century. Pope Francis's Year of Mercy is a call to each one of us to rediscover and to live the works of Mercy every day.

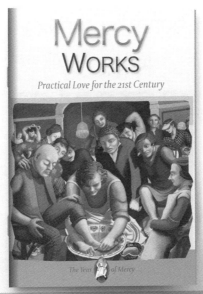

Spiritual Works of Mercy

Mgr Paul Grogan

Most Christians want to live an active faith yet feel perplexed about how to do so. The seven interconnected 'spiritual works of mercy' come to our aid: counselling the doubtful; instructing the ignorant; admonishing sinners; comforting the afflicted; forgiving offences; bearing wrongs patiently; and praying for the living and the dead. Through such acts of mercy we can respond fully to God's goodness towards us, involving conversion of our interior life: such acts are truly God's acts of mercy; we, mere human agents for God to alleviate people's unhappiness.

The Door of Mercy
in the words and life of Pope Francis

Fr Ivano Millico

The new 'Jubilee of Mercy' announced by Pope Francis is of great significance. Drawing from his biography, his motto, interviews, homilies, and messages, here we learn how Francis sees himself as a pilgrim in need of mercy. Further, we are all pilgrims, called to pass through the 'door of mercy' opening before us in this Holy Year. In a world that sits lightly to love and forgiveness, where many feel they are beyond forgiveness, this is an invitation to start out on a personal journey to discover what mercy truly is.

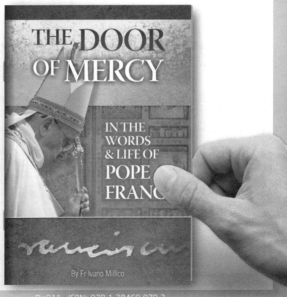

A world of Catholic reading at your fingertips...

Catholic Faith, Life & Truth for all

www.CTSbooks.org

twitter: @CTSpublishers

facebook.com/CTSpublishers

Catholic Truth Society, Publishers to the Holy See.